Poetic Philosophy Presents

Narrative Translations Designed for Accessibility

Seneca's Thyestes:

An Anima/Animus Tragedy of Pietas in Five Acts

By Seneca

I0171581

Translation and Stage Directions

by Jason Kassel, PhD

Recursive Publishing

Table of Contents

I. Made for You (1–175)

[Complete black. Silence. A sudden, jarring metallic clash. Across the audience, a single blinding white flash - like a lightning strike. Instant return to black.]

[Silence that lasts almost too long. A low, pulsing red light - slow, like a heartbeat - glows from beneath the stage. Then at once, violently brighter. From below, a single figure begins to rise - skeletal, gaunt, twitching. His jaw hangs in perpetual hunger. His limbs drag fog like seaweed. He does not arrive - he is disgorged. A thin vertical spotlight emerges on his face. Then slowly expands to his whole frame, backlit by the rising red glow.]

[As he rises, tapestries fall one by one from above - each displaying symbolic markers: a crowned lion, a shattered palace, an astrological chart, a river fork, a tree stripped of leaves, a map torn down its center. They remain suspended, swaying slightly.]

[Stage blacks out completely. Too long silence. Spotlight on the figure's face only. His mouth trembles, as if memory is just returning. The spotlight begins to expand outward, slowly revealing the ground beneath him, then his limbs, then the full stage. The red light fades as white and grey full - stage lighting sets the entire space as dim, liminal, decayed.]

[His arm extends upward. He stiffens, and slowly turns his face toward a new plane above. He shields his eyes as if struck by the light of memory - as if the very capacity to see were returning.]

Tantalus: Who rips me up from that cursed seat below - where I forever snap at fleeing food with jaws that never shut? Who dares show me again those god - filled halls, so ruinous once to see?

[He staggers. His limbs tremble. Then - collapse. A sudden gasp - as if Tartarus is exhaled from his chest and replaced by alien air.]

Is there some deeper curse than thirst beside the wave, or hunger, mouth agape, unending?

[He sinks to his knees. His body is dry - unable to weep.]

Must I now carry Sisyphus' slick, defiant stone along my back?

[His neck bows, chest caves, spine twisted like a hook.]

Will I be flung upon the wheel again? Lie like Tityos in his open cave - my guts a feast for black - winged birds that pluck by day what grows anew each night?

[He doubles forward in grief. A flicker of light plays across the audience - a signal that something is watching. He senses it. His body lifts - not by will, but by force. He now speaks not merely in anguish, but with prophetic terror.]

What new punishments are you writing into me?

[He knows he has crossed the threshold. He is now in a liminal state - a space between mortal and divine, between myth and reality.]

You - dark judge of shadows, who binds the dead in new torments - if there exists some suffering so vile even the jailer of Hell would tremble, some horror before which Acheron pales - then find it. Let even the damned fear it.

[Spotlight begins to constrict. Tantalus lowers his gaze, now facing forward - as if speaking to the world above. His tone changes - prophetic becomes infectious. He has become the carrier. This is no longer just lament - it is the return of something mythic.]

From my blood has risen a breed more monstrous than its fathers - a generation that dares what I dared not. They make me innocent.

[He collapses fully.]

Let me complete whatever impious place remains unfilled. So long as Pelops' house still stands, Minos shall never rest.

[Spotlight tightens to face. Then - blackout. Loud cymbalic clash. Stage black. Audience lights flicker violently - five flashes.]

[Suspended in flight above center stage: a Fury. Her hair writhes. Her eyes burn. A whip cracks in her hand. Shadows dance around her. She turns toward the audience

*- smile feral. As she speaks, she gestures - and audience -
actors erupt into chaos: shouting, accusations, being
dragged away by figures in modern security uniforms.]*

Fury: Go on, Accursed - Shade - infect your house.
Let every crime war with every other. Let every hand
draw blood.

[Spotlight strikes audience chaos.]

Let wrath know no limit. Let shame die. Let blind
madness jab their minds. Let the rage of parents rot into
the bones of their children.

*[She laughs. Cracks her whip. Her voice grows
liturgical.]*

Do not pause to hate what's already done - let new
crimes rise before the old ones cool.

*[At this, a large banner unfurls at the back of the
stage that reads, in bood red, "Let New Crimes Rise."]*

Not one sin in one man - but ten. And ten more.

*[Spotlights flash across the audience capturing
petty, eruptive outrages.]*

Let punishment grow the crime.

*[From above, mythic symbols fall: golden fleece,
sword, broken crown. They dangle, then are whisked away.
Replaced. Recycled.]*

Let kingship fall from proud brothers. Exile them
both. Let the throne pitch back and forth like a ship in an
endless storm.

[Echo from overhead speakers. Her lines reverberate:]

Let the mighty fall. [fall... fall...]

Let the fallen rise. [rise... rise...]

Let fate churn the throne in its tide. [tide... tide...]

[Cymbalic crash. Audience lights flicker 3x.]

[Images of Thyestes and his children project onto the back stage.]

When God brings the banished home - let them return to new crimes. And let all hate them - even themselves.

[A fan gently blows behind the "Let New Crimes Rise." banner.]

Let rage know no law. Let brother fear brother. Father dread his son. Son curse his father. Let their children perish - and worse - be born again.

[Projections end. Stage goes black. Beat. Audience lights glow. Behind the "Let New Crimes Rise." banner, the fan blows noticeably heavier. Four Fury doubles rise among the crowd, speaking in a united, disembodied voice - carried from overhead speakers.]

Fury Doubles: Let wives strike their husbands. Let war ride the waves. Let blood irrigate the land.

[Cymbal crash.]

Let Lust triumph over generals. Let rape be the least of crimes. Let Law, Faith, and Justice - all fall silent.

[Cymbal crash.]

Let Heaven itself be infected - Why do stars still shine in order? Why do fire - lights still adorn the sky? Let day fall from heaven. Let night reign.

[Cymbal crash.]

Let murder loose. And hatred. And funeral. And desecration. Let Tantalus' house be filled.

[Cymbal crash. Audience goes black. Beat. Full stage light returns. Fury spirals through air. Symbols descend and vanish in rapid succession. The fan blows behind the "Let New Crimes Rise." banner so hard it is extremely loud, and the words can't be read.]

Fury: Let the palace blaze with garlands. Crown the doors in laurel. Let joy bloom like poison. Let the hearth burn bright with pride. *[Stage black. Beat. Spotlight on Tantalus, still collapsed. Second spotlight reveals Fury hovering again.]*

Why do you still hesitate?

[The overhead speakers reverberate "you....you...you"]

Let the feast begin. Thyestes does not yet weep - but he will. Oh yes - he will.

[Dual spotlights remain. Audience lights come on. Symbols fall. Fury slowly descends. Breaks the fourth wall. The fan stops blowing behind the "Let New Crimes Rise." banner. Reverberated "you....you...you" repeats in a low - conversational volume.]

The pots boil. Limbs are sorted. An uncle's hearth shall drink a nephew's blood. Set the banquet.

[The "Let New Crimes Rise." banner lifts.]

You are no stranger to this crime. It was always yours. This day - this hunger - was made for you.

[At this line, a cup of wine with a "Made for You," card descends onto each audience member's lap.]

Drink - and know your blood is in the wine. The feast you tried to flee - I've found it.

[Long silence. All lights cut to black. Beat. Spotlight shows tapestry with blood - red lettering falling in sequence:]

"But wait,

To where

Are you rushing,

[Final tapestry:]

Tantalus' soul?"

[This tapestry expands horizontally so that the words and question mark cover the entire back with a spotlight. Audience lights remain glowing. Audience lights fade to blackout. Stage in complete darkness. All banners are lifted. Reverberated "you....you...you" ends.]

[Projections of the underworld appear at the back of the stage. A single spotlight strikes Tantalus. A red underglow pulses beneath him. He remains skeletal - clutching at the air, as if clawing his way back into the underworld. He stands on a circular revolve, oriented stage

- left. The revolve begins a slow, mechanical ascent, lifting approximately 10 inches to reveal a hollow void beneath - lit subtly in red. At its apex, the motion subtly accelerates - not jarring, but deliberate. When Tantalus faces directly downstage, he begins to speak. His gestures strain toward despair, but his frame is too depleted - he reaches for tears he cannot produce.]

Tantalus: Take me back - to the stagnant pools and backward - flowing streams, to the vanishing water and the fruit that flees my lips! Let me return to the black prison - bed that was mine. If I seem not miserable enough - then let me change rivers, let me be abandoned midstream in your fire - fed channel, Phlegethon, ringed by flames.

[The underworld projections are now appearing in audience - adjacent walls as well as on stage. The revolve continues its slow rotation toward stage - right. It completes one full counter - clockwise revolution. At the completion of the first 360°, the rotation accelerates slightly - still steady, but no longer ghostlike.]

[A female child walks in front of the stage, and among the audience, with a sign too large for her to carry that says "You."]

You - all of you who suffer the punishments that Fate decrees - who tremble in hollow caves, awaiting the mountain's fall - who face the jaws of lions or the whips of howling Furies - half - burnt souls who fend off flying brands - hear me! I, Tantalus, call out, rushing toward you.

[As he speaks, the revolve spins faster. His voice comes from overhead speakers.]

Believe me - I have risen - I speak as one who knows: Love your torments, for when shall I ever escape this Above - World?

[The girl with the You card disappears.]

[The revolve continues its counter - clockwise rotation, with him spinning in uninterrupted circles. Above, a second spotlight ignites: a Fury is suspended in midair. She begins to circle slowly overhead. Her orbit traces a tightening predatory spiral above the revolve. As the Fury's voice enters, large symbolic props begin to descend visibly from above - banners, broken standards, and tattered tapestries bearing cryptic inscriptions or ancestral curses. Each object drops on a clearly visible wire.]

[Tantalus spins steadily counter - clockwise, his posture increasingly urgent - arms outstretched, as if reaching downward, straining toward the underworld. The revolve begins to lower. She flies and screeches maniacally.]

Fury: No! First, confound your house. Bring war into it. And with it - teach kings to crave the blade. Shake their savage chests with turmoil - until they split themselves.

[As her last lines land, the revolve - still lifted but descending and spinning counter - clockwise - begins to traverse the stage laterally. It glides slowly along an embedded track, dragging Tantalus with it as though he were chained to fate itself.]

[The symbolic props continue to fall - each one heavier, darker, stranger. The air becomes increasingly crowded with signs of ruin. In a spotlight, flying, the Fury erupts - snapping her whip, flinging shadows, shrieking with rage. Her tantrum is aerial and volatile.]

Tantalus: It is right that I suffer punishment - not become the punishment. Am I to rise like a vapor, unleashed from the ruptured earth - a plague blown across cities? Am I to become the ancestral torch that guides my grandchildren into horror? O great Father of gods - yes, ours, though I am shamed to say it - even if my words are cursed, and my tongue tortured for speaking them, I will not be silent: I warn them - Do not stain sacred hands with blood. Do not defile the altars with madness.

I will stand, I will resist the crime!

[The "Let New Crimes Rise." banner rises, then the spotlight on Fury goes black. Three embedded cast - audience members scream. The cries are staggered, not simultaneous and are in different locations. On stage, a single white spotlight pins Tantalus in place until a deafening mechanical SNAP results in full stage blackout.

Above the audience, a lightening flash of light, flooding the house in a flash of unnatural exposure. Full stage lights return, and the revolve visibly jerks to a halt - hard, sudden, and final - facing directly forward. Tantalus is frozen mid-motion.]

[Across the stage scrim or rear wall, a massive projection appears: the face of the Fury, beaming. Her smile is too wide, too calm - radiant with triumph, or madness.]

[The girl with the too - large You card returns and walks among the audience.]

Why do you snap your whips at me? Why do you threaten me with twisted snakes?

[The Fury laughs through speakers hung above the audience.]

Why do you stir that hunger already nailed into my marrow? My heart blazes with thirst. My guts seethe like fire.

[The revolve begins to move clockwise and ascend.]

I follow.

[Complete blackout.]

[Tight spotlight on Fury flying above the stage. A pin of light slowly expands, starting with his face, on Tanatalus, until it is a complete spotlight. As Fury speaks her line, food descends and Tantalus eats greedily.]

Fury: Yes - take that Fury and pour it through your line! Let them rage. Let them thirst for each other's blood.

Your house already feels your entrance. It recoils. It shudders. That is enough - Return now to your pit, to the stream you know.

[Revolve begins rotating clockwise and descends, the food is lifted out of Tantalus' reach. Loud ocean sounds emit from overhead speakers.]

Already the grieving earth sinks beneath your foot. See - the spring's water turns inward. The banks are dry. The fire - wind scatters what clouds remain. All trees grow pale. Their branches, stripped, thirst as the fruit vanishes.

[Tantalus has fully descended and all that is visible is red pulsating light from beneath the stage.]

Even the Isthmus - surging between two seas - now stands in stunned silence, listening to distant waves from lands far off.

[Blackout. Ocean sounds stop. Fury face is projected onto backstage.]

Lerna dries. Phoronis' veins collapse. Alpheus withholds his sacred flow. Cithaeron's slopes - snowless, bare - stand in fear. And the noble plains of Argos fear again the thirst of old.

[Lights over audience come on. Children appear with meat appetizers and glasses of wine. Sound continues to come from overhead speakers.]

Behold - even Titan falters. He hesitates - whether to pull the sun behind him and drag the day into death.

[Complete Blackout.]

[Blackness. Small spotlights on puppets portraying the gods lowered from above the stage. In the back of the stage, projections of life on the island of Argos are seen - children playing, peaceful fields, laurel crowns. The tone is idealized but fragile. Once the puppets are fully lowered, the stage lights come on. The stage is empty. The Chorus, a disembodied older male voice, emits though overhead speakers.]

Chorus [Dis - Embodied Old Man]: If any of the gods above still loves the land of Argos, and its Achaean bloodline, its Pisaean halls famed for chariots - If any still favors the Isthmian throne of Corinth, with its twin harbors and the sea split into warring tides - If anyone delights in Taygetus' shining snows, which icy Boreas, in his Sarmatian winter Fury, piled upon its peaks - and which the sailing Etesian winds melt again beneath summer's sun - If any spirit, touched by the bright stream of Alpheus, famed in the Olympic stadium, still guards this place with gentle power - then turn your gaze this way.

[All of the theater lights come on. Two beats. Blackout. Projected images continue: joyful Argive youth, festivals, games. Spotlight reveals an older man - clearly old, but neither elder nor frail. He wears contemporaneous Noble - Attire, and speaks with Aristocratic - Poise.]

Chorus [Embodied Old Man]: Hold back the cursed flood of crimes reborn. Let not each sin return greater in the grandson than in the grandfather. Let some ending come to the madness in the line of Tantalus - a race of impious ruin. Let it be enough - Enough has been sinned.

[Spotlight fades until black. Sound continues from overhead speakers.]

No sacred law held. No shared humanity preserved. The master's trust betrayed, Myrtilus slain by deception - his blood staining the sea that now bears his name. No tale is more known among Ionian ships.

[Spotlight returns to the Old Man. Overhead speakers repeat in increasing layers: "Everyone knows. Everyone knows."]

A child - rushing to his father's embrace - caught instead a murderer's blade. Too young for the hearth, he was cut down in sacrifice. And you, Tantalus - with your own hand, you divided your son's flesh to lay it on the table before the gods, your guests.

[Audience lights dim, and children appear among the audience with roasted - meat and glasses of wine. Sound continues to come from overhead speakers.]

Chorus (Dis-Embodied Old Man): That meat - eternally hungers after you. That drink - eternally thirsts within you. No punishment could better fit the horror of that feast.

[Stage blackout. Audience blackout. Stage lights return. Now onstage: a children as chorus, dressed in identical contemporaneous middle - society uniforms. Each stands on a small riser. They hold cue cards and read from them in slow, careful rhythm. In front of them, backs turned toward the audience, stand rows of silent adults in contemporaneous middle - society clothing. As the children recite, the adults break eye contact. One after another, until they are facing the audience in shame while the children speak.]

Chorus (Embodied - Children): Tantalus stands, worn out, his throat a hollow of thirst. Above his guilty head, a thousand dooms hang - yet even they are swifter to vanish than the prey of Phineus' starving birds. Around him, trees bend low, laden with heavy fruit - boughs curved, trembling, brushing against his open mouth. Still, though desperate and impatient, he fails to grasp them - fooled again and again, he turns his eyes away, clenches his mouth, and chains his hunger inside locked teeth.

But then - as if the grove takes pity - the entire orchard leans in, gently dropping soft fruit onto his outstretched arms. The leaves caress his face like mercy. They inflame the hunger anew. They stir his hands - but the moment he reaches - the moment he believes - Autumn itself is torn skyward, the forest vanishes into wind.

Then thirst comes - not lesser than his hunger, but crueler still. And when his blood boils with fiery thirst, when his mouth blazes as if lit by torches - he stands, gaping, reaching for the waves rushing toward him - but the fleeing water draws back into dry rock, and the river vanishes. The flood he chases betrays him again.

Instead of drinking - he gulps a mouthful of dust from the deep, retreating whirlpool.

[Blackout. Stage and audience lights return. Now seen onstage: a wide banner drops down in blood - red lettering:]

"Children learned history. Are adults watching?"

[After ten seconds of silence and stillness - all lights to black.]

II. A Decision and a Celebration (176–403)

[The stage lights come on. In front of the stage, on a track, is a metal image of a man facing backwards holding a glowing sun orb. The track moves the backwards figure in an Eastern direction. Midway, the orb dims and shifts to a silver moon mask. This procession loops throughout the scene, repeating slowly, unnaturally.]

[The stage is a throne room with a massive blackened bronze throne in the back. It is angular, and cold, sitting raised on a crimson marble dais. The throne must be exited

sideways and, in doing so, pieces of clothing always get caught.]

[Atreas sits and rises repeatedly. He rises, paces the stage in a line along the throne's edge, and then reenters the throne with ritual stiffness. His pacing mirrors the rising sun: restless, obsessive, caught in the same loop.]

[In center stage there is a large human - height model of Capitoline Hill, constructed like a miniature fortress. Atop it stands a puppet - scale Temple of Jupiter with hinged bronze doors. Scattered in front of it are 3 - foot puppets - clay or bronze - cast Roman gods in vivid armor: Jupiter, Mars, Bellona, Apollo.]

[Satalles, the Attendant, is crouched near the model, manipulating the gods as he speaks. His motions are exaggerated, fawning, dramatic, drawing the gods into postures of war, judgment, or accusation. Whenever Fury is invoked, he swings Mars' puppet in a circle, dragging a flaming chariot across the Capitoline model. When Atreus expresses doubt or hesitation, hepresses Jupiter's puppet down into the throne. For each imagined atrocity, he manipulates the puppets into attacking invisible enemies - slaughter scenes played out in eerie silence, only the clash of wood on bronze audible.]

[On the stage, over the actors and props, is a projection of Thyestes and Aeropes in a passionate embrace. On the edges of the stage are court painters whose canvases can be clearly seen. They are all painting *the same thing - the same Aeropes and Thyestes in a passionate embrace as the projection. They clearly take orders from Satelles.]*

Satelles: Coward. Slothful. Spiritless. And - worst shame for a ruler in peril - unavenged. After all your brother's crimes, after his betrayals, after he's torn all sacred law to shreds - do you stand here, Atreus, growling useless laments?

You should have already made the whole earth thunder with your armies. The twin seas should be roaring with fleets - flames should devour his lands, his cities should glow in ruin, blades should gleam in every hand, and all Argos should ring with war - cries.

No forest should shield him. No mountaintop fortress should stand. Let the whole Mycenaean people rise with a single call to arms. Whoever harbors that hated head, let them fall in the ruin he brings.

[Satelles swings the Mars puppet's sword so violently, the model Capitoline Hill cracks down the center. One half collapses forward - toward the audience. He hurriedly and guiltily patches it, binding it with red cord.]

Even this great and storied house of Pelops - let it collapse, even on me, so long as it falls on him.

Now - stir your soul to something no future age will praise, but none will dare ignore. Do some unspeakable crime. Some wild, blood - drenched deed so monstrous your brother himself would have claimed it.

[Satelles runs offstage, quickly returns with a new 'child king' puppet on a miniature altar, and places it into the puppet temple, shutting the doors.]

Don't settle for petty revenge. Conquer him in horror. What cruelty could surpass his?

Is he groveling now? Has he ever shown restraint in good fortune - or mercy when fortune failed? I know the man. He cannot be bent. He can only be broken. So - before he gathers his strength, before he braces himself - strike first. Better to attack the sleeping beast than be hunted while you rest.

It's kill or be killed. The crime sits in the middle - waiting for the one who dares.

[The overhead speakers play laughter at a very loud volume, then it slowly becomes steady at the sound of a low conversation.]

But does the public's judgment mean nothing to you?

[All of the court painters stop and look at Atreus.]

Atreus: That's the greatest gift of kingship - your people are forced not only to endure what you do, but to praise it.

[Painters return to work.]

Satelles: Fear can make men speak praise - but it makes them enemies all the same. He who seeks true glory wants honor from the heart, not just from the lips.

Atreus: True praise finds the humble. False praise comes only to the powerful, because people pretend to love what they fear.

Satelles: A good king should want what is right. And if he does, the people will want the same.

Atreus: Where only what is right is permitted to rulers, then rule itself is borrowed - not owned.

Satelles: Without shame, without justice, without sanctity or trust - no kingdom can last.

Atreus: Sanctity. Trust. Justice. Piety. These are private virtues. Let kings walk a sharper path.

Satelles: But surely even against a wicked brother, to do harm is wrong?

[Stage goes black. Spotlight on Atreus who paces without speaking. Projection of Atreus' face speaking words. Sound comes from overhead speakers.]

Atreus: Whatever is forbidden in a brother - is permitted in that brother. What crime did he ever hold back from? He raped my wife. He stole my throne. He seized imperial dignity by deceit and shattered my house with it.

In the sacred stalls of Pelops, there was a wondrous beast - a golden - fleeced ram, leader of a majestic flock. Gold poured down his entire coat, a symbol of kingship: from his back came the golden scepters of Tantalus' line. Whoever holds that ram - rules. Fate binds the kingdom to that creature. Set apart, it grazed the sacred meadow within stone walls, guarded behind a fated rock.

And this - this was the sacred beast my brother dared steal, with my wife as his accomplice. From that crime all ruin poured forth: mutual destruction, exile, fear, every corner of my bloodline stalked by plots.

My marriage - poisoned. My reign - shaken. My house - sick. Even my children - uncertain blood. Only one truth is sure: my brother is my enemy.

Why do you hesitate? At last - Begin! Summon your courage. Look back at Tantalus. Look at Pelops. These hands were born to follow such examples.

[Audience lights come on. Stage lights come on.]

Now tell me: Through what terrible path shall I strike his head?

[Blackout.]

[Stage lights come on.]

Satelles: Strike him down with steel, let his cursed breath be forced out in death.

Atreus: You speak of ends. I want punishment. A soft tyrant grants death - In my kingdom, death must be begged for.

Satelles: Does no sense of kinship or pity move you?

Atreus: Be gone, Piety - if you were ever a guest in this house! Let the dread sisterhood of Furies come instead. Let discordant Erinys arrive, Let Megaera swing her twin torches in wrath. My chest is ablaze - but not enough. Let it swell, filled with a monster even greater.

Satelles: What new madness are you crafting?

Atreus: Nothing that can be contained by ordinary pain. No crime will be spared. And no crime will be enough.

Satelles: Steel?

Atreus: Too mild.

Satelles: Fire, then?

Atreus: Still not enough.

Satelles: What weapon could such pain ever find?

Atreus: Thyestes - himself.

Satelles: That's no longer anger - it's something worse.

Atreus: I confess it: A storm pounds my soul, shakes it to its depths. I'm swept up - Where? I don't know. But I'm swept.

[From both left and right, fans blow strong air into the audience. Natural sounds mimicking the script emit from overhead speakers.]

The earth groans from its base. Clear skies thunder. The house shudders as if shattered to its roof. Even the household gods avert their faces. Let it be done. Let the crime unfold - Even you, gods, shall tremble.

[He smashes the puppet - gods.]

Satelles: What in heaven's name are you planning?

[The painters are shooed out of the throne - room by Satelles. Atreus caresses the canvas images while speaking.]

Atreus: I don't know, but something greater than thought, something beyond the boundary of human custom, presses against my idle hands. I cannot name it - but it is a kind of avalanche.

[Stage goes black. Spotlight on Atreus who paces without speaking. Projection of Atreus' face speaking words. Sound comes from overhead speakers.]

So be it. Claim it, soul! A crime worthy of Thyestes, and worthy of Atreus - the kind of crime each could commit. The tables of Thrace have witnessed such feasts. Yes - what I plan is monstrous. But it has been done. So pain must find something worse. Inspire me now, Mother of Baulis - my ancestress! And you, my sister - our cause is the same. Stand with me. Push my hand forward!

Let the ravenous father delight as he devours his children's flesh. Yes - this will do. This will suffice.

So - where is he? Why has Atreus wandered innocent for so long? Already the whole image of the slaughter dances before my eyes. I see it - Fatherhood crammed back into the father's mouth.

So, soul - why flinch? Why retreat before the act? We must dare.

[Audience lights come on. Stage lights come on.]

And let the worst of this crime - be done by Thyestes' own hand.

[*Blackout. Stage lights come on.*]

Satelles: But by what trick will you drag him into the snare? He believes all things hostile.

Atreus: He could not be trapped - unless he wanted to be. Now he hopes for my kingdom. It is with that hope that he will march into Jove's own thunderbolt, sail across the storms of swollen seas, brave the peril of Syrtes and Libyan shoals. It is with that hope - which he thinks is his greatest terror - that he shall see his brother.

Satelles: Who would ever trust peace? Who could believe such terms?

Atreus: False hope is always credulous. But we'll send a message - carried by his own sons. Let them go, Let them bear this message to their uncle. Let the exile, long wandering from every hearth, trade his suffering for rule.

Let him reign, half of Argos in his grasp. If Thyestes resists - too proud for supplication - his children, innocent and weary of their long suffering, will soften him with their prayers. From one side - the madness of old kingship. From the other - poverty, hardship, toil. These shall break him down - this man long hardened by misfortune.

Satelles: Surely now, after all these years, his suffering must feel lighter?

Atreus: You're wrong. The weight of sorrow increases with time. To endure misery is far worse than to suffer it.

Satelles: Then find another to serve as agent in this dreadful plot.

Atreus: The young obey harsh commands more readily.

Satelles: But whatever you teach them to do to their uncle - they may turn against you. Even the teacher of crime can become its victim.

Atreus: Even if no one teaches treachery, a throne itself teaches it. You're afraid they'll become monsters?

They are born monsters.

That thing you call cruelty - that roughness, that impiety - perhaps they already carry it within them.

Satelles: Do they know what deception you intend?

Atreus: No. Children that young have no instinct for secrecy. They might reveal the plan. Silence is a skill taught only by suffering.

Satelles: But won't you, by trying to deceive another, also deceive your own sons?

[Stage goes black. Spotlight on Atreus who paces without speaking. Projection of Atreus' face speaking words. Sound comes from overhead speakers.]

Atreus: Let them remain innocent - blameless. Why drag them into my crime? Let my hatred do its own work, through me alone. You hesitate again, soul? If you spare your sons - you'll spare his sons too. No - let Agamemnon knowingly serve this plan. Let Menelaus help avenge his father, and from this crime, let the question of their birth be confirmed. If they resist - if they plead peace, if they call him "uncle" - he is still a father. Let them go. But beware: a trembling face reveals what the heart would hide. Reluctance betrays great schemes.

[Audience lights come on. Stage lights come on.]

If they know too much - our plot dies.

[Black. Stage lights come on.]

Satelles: You needn't convince me. Both fear and loyalty live in me. But I will keep this loyalty tightly sealed.

[Blackout.]

[Stage lights rise. The back wall is lit with a projection of the citadel of Argos - steep stone stairs, distant hills, high ramparts. At center stage stands a worn stone platform before the palace gates. Vendors and townspeople move through the agora, murmuring, transacting.]

[Enter the Town-Crier. He moves deliberately, ringing a handbell with each step. He climbs the platform. In his hands: a wooden tablet etched with wax, a metal stylus. A leather satchel hangs at his side, filled with scrolls. He pauses, scanning the crowd. The bell ceases. The crowd gathers, or turns toward him in silence.]

Crier (Chorus): So - at last - the noble house, descended from Inachus, has calmed the storm between brothers.

[The crowd erupts in cheers. Children appear in the aisles throwing confetti, blowing horns. The projection slowly dissolves - from the citadel of Argos to towering statues of the gods. A moment of awe. The crier raises one hand. The noise halts.]

Crier (Chorus): And yet - what madness drives you still?

To spill blood for blood?

To seize the throne by crime?

You who hunger for high towers -

know not where true kingship lies.

[Staggered cries of "Hail Zeus!" erupt from the stage and cast-audience. The crier turns, steps forward, points toward them.]

Crier (Chorus): A king is not made by wealth,

nor by Tyrian-dyed robes,

nor by the gleam of a diadem,

nor beams of gold upon palace rafters.

The king is he who casts off fear,

who rules the deep chaos of his heart.

No lust for power,

no shifting wind of popular favor shall move him.

[The crier finishes. He scans the crowd one last time. He packs his things slowly. A silence follows. The cheers do

not return. He exits. The vendors resume their trading, as if nothing had been said.]

[Three children walk onto the stage and climb the platform. The crowd does not see them. They stand in stillness. Their unified voices echo from above, spoken through overhead speakers.]

Children (Chorus): Not all the gold the West can dig,

>nor Tagus' golden stream,
>
>nor Libya's burning threshing floors,
>
>nor sudden bolts from crooked skies -
>
>Not gales that churn the seas,
>
>nor the wild rage of Adria's tide,
>
>nor soldier's lance,
>
>nor naked steel...
>
>The king is he who stands in peace
>
>and sees all things below him.
>
>He welcomes fate.
>
>He does not complain to die.

[A spotlight shines on a man standing in the audience. He does not move. A solemn adult male voice is heard through the overhead speakers.]

Male (Chorus): Let those rule who must over distant Dabas,

>or the red shores of the East,
>
>or jeweled seas dyed with blood -
>
>let them control the Caspian heights,

and the wild tribes of Sarmatia.

Let him cross the ford of Danube,

or seek the distant Seres with their noble silk.

He needs no horse. No arms.

No coward's dart like the Parthian feigns.

No engines of war to hurl stone at distant cities.

The good mind possesses the kingdom.

The king is he who fears nothing.

The king is he who desires nothing.

(Beat)

This kingdom - each man gives to himself.

[A spotlight shines on a woman standing in the audience. She remains still. A quiet adult female voice is heard from the speakers.]

Female (Chorus): Let others stand atop palace spires,

shivering on slippery heights.

Let me be fed by sweet tranquility.

Let me dwell in a quiet place,

in gentle peace.

Let my name remain unknown to the Roman crowd.

Let my days pass by in silence.

Let me die - an old man among the people.

Death weighs heavy on the man too known by others -

yet forever a stranger to himself.

[The statues of the gods fade. The citadel of Argos returns. One child on the platform turns to face the audience. Blackout.]

III. Instructions, Promises, and Circles (404–626)

[Stage lights rise. At center stage stands a ceremonial carriage, drawn and flanked by a formal retinue: attendants, guards, and children in noble attire. Behind them, the projection on the back wall shifts - the city of Argos appears: high stone walls, palace gates, olive-covered hills bathed in Mediterranean light.]

[Throughout this dialogue, from stage right, people walk backwards across the stage carrying sandwich boards (SB) inscribed with Latin terms. Each board is echoed by an overhead speaker with an English voiceover. They move slowly but are ignored by the retinue, by Thyestes, and by Tantalus - as if unseen. They pass like thoughts. Or omens.]

Thyestes: The longed-for roofs of my homeland -

[SB: Optata, Overhead Speaker: "Longed-for."]

The ancient wealth -

[SB: Opes, Overhead Speaker: "Wealth."]

The highest blessing for an exile -

[SB: Summum Bonum, Overhead Speaker: "Ultimate Good."]

The sight of my native soil -

[Two walkers move apart accordion-style to reveal SB: Soli Natalis, Overhead Speaker: "Native Soil."]

And ancestral gods -

[Projection of Thyestes' face appears in a circular halo behind him. Echoed by overhead speakers.]

(if gods there still are...).

[Projection vanishes.]

I see the towers the Cyclopes raised, built with toil beyond human strength.

[SB: Cyclopum Turris, Overhead Speaker: "Towers of Giants"]

There! The stadiums - celebrated in my youth -

[SB: Palmam, Overhead Speaker: "Victory"]

where I drove my father's chariot to glorious victory.

[SB: Currus Paternus, Overhead Speaker: "Father's Chariot"]

All Argos will come running - the people will greet me.

[Blackout. Spotlight on Thyestes who doesn't move or speak. Circular projection of Thyestes face appears. Overhead speakers. Side speakers emit Nature noises at a low volume.]

But so will Atreus. No. Better to return to the wilderness, the thickets, the animals. A life more honest in its savagery. This kingdom's dazzling light is no true glory. It blinds the eyes - but only with falsehood. And when you gaze at the gift - look too at the giver.

Once, when I lived among hardship, I was strong - almost cheerful. Now I am thrown into fear again. My soul retreats, pulls my body back, and each step feels against my will.

[Nature sounds end. Projection ends. Spotlight goes black. Stage Lights come on.]

Tantalus: Father, why do you hesitate - staring like a statue, your face turning away, frozen in uncertainty?

[SB: Quid Hoc Est?, Overhead Speaker: "What is this?"]

[Blackout. Spotlight on Thyestes who doesn't move or speak. Circular projection of Thyestes face appears. Overhead speakers.]

Thyestes: Why do you tremble, soul? Why do you twist your resolve so easily? You trust what is most uncertain - a brother, a throne - yet fear evils that are past and run from sufferings well endured?

It was better to be in exile. Turn around, while you still can.

[Projection ends. Spotlight goes black. Stagelights come on.]

Tantalus: But what makes you pause, Father? Why recoil from such wonders? Your brother's wrath has ended - he restores half the kingdom, and begins to mend our fractured house.

He restores you to yourself.

[Projection of Thyestes' face appears but doesn't speak. Thyestes on stage speaks and moves and emits sound. Nature sounds emit from overhead speakers. Throughout people, without SB:, walk backwards in front of and behind Thyestes.]

Thyestes: You ask the cause of my fear - when I myself do not know it. There is nothing visible to fear, yet still, I fear. My legs want to go, but fail beneath me. I try to walk forward - and find myself pulled elsewhere. Like a ship pushed forward by oars and sail, yet drawn back by a tide that resists both.

[Stage empties except for Tantalus and Thyestes. As a servant exits, he hands Tantalus a crown which he takes, walks towards Thyestes, and offers to place it on his head. Stage goes black except for spotlights on the two who are stationary. Stage is structured so Tantalus is situated noticeably higher than Thyestes.]

Tantalus: Overcome it - whatever blocks your soul. See what prizes await your return. You can be king again.

Thyestes: I can also choose to die.

Tantalus: But the summit of power -

[Thyestes, back to the audience, gazes at the projection of Argos.]

Thyestes: - is no power at all, if you desire nothing.

[Seeing that Thyestes has his back turned, Tantalus tries on the crown.]

Tantalus: You'll leave it to your sons?

Thyestes: A kingdom cannot hold two.

Tantalus: Would you rather suffer than seize happiness?

[Thyestes looks at Tantalus, who quickly hides his actions and extends the crown. A circular projection of Thyestes' face appears and stays on throughout the entire monologue alternating between Thyestes on stage speaking and sound emitting from overhead speakers.]

Thyestes' Face: Believe me: greatness is but a name. Hardship is feared in vain. When I stood highest - I never ceased to fear. I feared the very blade at my own side.

Thyestes speaks to Tantalus: Oh, how sweet is this: to stand in no one's way, to eat safely on the ground. Crime doesn't enter huts. A small table feeds the whole family. But poison is drunk from golden cups - I know it.

Thyestes' Face: I would rather have a cursed fate than a golden one. Not the palace that looms atop the highest cliff, nor the one that terrifies the humble towns below, nor the ceilings gilded in ivory, nor guards that protect the sleepless.

Thyestes speaks to Tantalus: We don't fish with fleets. We don't drive back the sea with walls of stone. We don't feed a greedy belly by taxing nations.

Thyestes' Face: No fields of mine stretch past the Getae or the Parthians.

Thyestes speaks to Tantalus: We don't offer incense to the gods, nor deck our altars with gold while Jupiter is barred from the house. No forests perch atop our roofs. No steaming lakes boil from our hand. No days are yoked to sleepless nights in wine - soaked vigil.

Thyestes' Face: Yes - power is given. But no one fears me.

Thyestes speaks to Tantalus: My house is safe, even without weapons. And in small things - I find great peace. To endure without ruling - that is a kingdom vast beyond all thrones.

Tantalus: If the gods offer you a throne, you should not refuse it - but neither should you seek it. Your brother asks that you reign.

Thyestes' Face: He asks? Then I must fear. Where there is a request, a trick often hides.

Tantalus: But Piety returns to the very house that once exiled it. A Just Love can regain its strength.

Thyestes' Face: Does my brother love me? The sea will wash the northern stars before that day comes. Sicily's greedy tides will freeze mid - wave, wheat will grow from Ionian waves, and black night will shine like the sun - flames will mix with floods, life with death, storms will strike a bargain with the sea - before Atreus loves me.

Tantalus: But what trick could you possibly fear?

Thyestes' Face: Every kind. What limit could I ever place on his hatred? He can do as much harm as he holds hatred.

Tantalus: But what can he do to you now?

Thyestes to Tantalus: I no longer fear for myself - it's you. You make me fear Atreus.

Tantalus: So, caution will get you caught?

Thyestes' Face: Caution comes too late when you're already in the jaws of ruin.

Thyestes to Tantalus: Let's go then - but hear this, my son: I follow you, not lead.

Tantalus: A good heart will draw the favor of the gods. Go - step forward without fear.

[Blackout.]

[Stage lights are very dark. Spotlight on Atreus who is standing on a platform and speaking to the audience. On the back-stage, are two projections. One is a scene of Thyestes and children arriving. A second is a circular image in which Atreus' face appears and, when speaking, sound emits from overhead speakers.]

Atreus (Face): The beast is in the cage - trapped just as I placed it. I see both Thyestes and his sons - that whole cursed breed, a chain of blood linked to him.

At last - at last! Thyestes is mine. He has walked straight into my hands, intact, unaware. I can barely restrain myself. My Fury bursts its leash! Just like a hunting dog, leashed too long, who sniffs the trail and feels the nearness of prey - still held back, still quiet - but once the boar is close, he strains, growls, and nearly rips himself free from his master's grip. So too does rage, when it tastes blood - it cannot hide itself, even when told to.

But - let it hide, for now. See how his face - withered in sorrow - is buried beneath unkempt hair, how his beard lies filthy on his chest? Let this look of sorrow play its part. I will act the brother. Let me see him, embrace him, welcome him back.

[Atreus exits platform and platform is removed from stage. Projection of the outside arrival scene ends. When Thyestes and his children enter, a second circular projection appears with Thyestes' face that speaks through overhead speakers.]

Atreus (Spoken): Let the rage rest. From this day forward - let there be blood and family, let enmity die.

Thyestes (Spoken): If you were not like this, Atreus - I would confess my crimes.

Theyestes (Face): Yes, I confess: everything you've accused me of, I did. My cause is wretched - but it is Piety itself that compels me now. And in your eyes, that makes me most guilty.

[Thyestes and his children kneel.]

Thyestes (Spoken): I kneel to you. Let my innocent hands, never raised in violence, speak for me. Let the rage be wiped away. Let the swelling hatred vanish.

[Thyestes and children rise. He stands behind the children and pushes them forward.]

Thyestes (Spoken): Take these children - my pledge of trust.

[Atreus gestures towards guards who take the children to the front stage right. There the children are massaged with various oils and rubbed with herbs.]

Atreus (Spoken): No need to kneel. Give me your arms - embrace me. And you - my strength, these noble sons - cling to my neck! Tear off those rags! Let your eyes be spared that sorrow. Put on garments that match your royal place. Rejoice - not in my rule, but in your share of it.To restore a brother's crown - that is a greater glory than to keep it. To hold a throne is Fortune. To give it - Virtue.

Thyestes (Spoken): May the gods return to you, brother, a reward equal to the gift you offer me. But look - this soiled robe rejects the mark of royalty. And these hands - ruined by exile - should not touch the scepter. et me hide among the crowd - let me be no one.

Atreus (Spoken): This kingdom has room for two.

[Blackout. Spotlight on Tantalus. He holds a card that says, "Didn't Thyestes just say a kingdom couldn't hold two?" Blackout. Lights on.]

Thyestes (Spoken): Then I will believe that all you have is mine.

[Atreus' Face speaks - sound emitting from overhead speaker - simultaneously with actor onstage.]

Atreus (Spoken): And who turns down gifts from Fortune's flowing hand?

[Thyestes' Face speaks - sound emitting from overhead speaker - simultaneously with actor onstage.]

Thyestes (Spoken): He who has seen how fast they vanish.

Atreus (Spoken): Will you deny me the glory of crowning my own brother?

Thyestes (Spoken): Your glory is already complete. Now it's my turn - to reject the throne.

Thyestes (Face): That is my resolve.

Atreus (Spoken): If you refuse your share, then I will renounce mine.

Thyestes (Spoken): I accept - but only the title of king, not the rights or the weapons. They remain yours.

Atreus (Spoken): Then wear the crown on that venerable brow. And I -

[Atreus walks over to the children and calls a guard to take them. When they are offstage he speaks.]

I will go and offer the destined victims to the gods.

[Blackout.]

[Lights rise. Center stage is framed by a still projection of the City of Argos - bright, idealized, almost static. A civic crowd bustles in silence: families, vendors, children. Every figure holds or wears a circle - bags, hats,

shields, trays - marking them as participants in a world of cycles. This background remains still, unchanging.]

[On the far left and far right, two flat panels slowly rise from the stage floor, like emerging thoughts. Each bears a mounted petaurum - springboards. Beneath each is etched in projected light: "Epistulae Morales ad Lucilium 15.3." A single man stands on the left platform. He bounces, launches, somersaults. He lands on the right, and without pause, repeats. No applause. The crowd does not notice.]

[After 3x Beats, the projection of Argos shifts to a collection of adults wearing the Mask of Tragedy. They speak in unison and their voices emit from overhead speakers. As they speak, children walk through the audience with grill carts on which they grill meat. Others provide wine.]

Chorus (Disembodied in Unison): Who would believe it? That savage man - that tyrant, Atreus - stood dumbstruck at the sight of his brother.

[The Chorus figures bow and rise.]

There is no force greater than true Piety.

[The Chorus figures bow and rise.]

Hatred may rage between strangers, but those once bound by true love - they will remain bound. Even when wrath flares, and storms tear old bonds, and the war - horns scream - Piety still finds a way to pull back the sword. When brother faces brother, and the blood calls, and the battlefield trembles - yet Piety enters, and clasped hands quench the fire of steel.

[All of the people on stage turn to the audience and say]: What god has made such peace from such chaos?

Chorus (Disembodied in Unison): Just now, Mycenae rang with war's clamor. Pale mothers clutched their sons. Wives shrank back from war- drenched husbands. Blades were drawn, but the fighters hesitated.

[All of the people on stage turn to the audience and say]: They were ashamed of peace.

Chorus (Disembodied in Unison): Walls had begun to crumble. Gates braced with iron. Watchmen clung to the towers. Night was thick with fear.

[All of the people on stage turn to the audience and say]: Worse than war is the fear of war.

[Except for Chorus projection, stage black. From this point forward, Nature Sounds, at conversational level, emit from side-speakers.]

Chorus (Disembodied in Unison): But now - the blades fall silent. The horns no longer scream. Mycenae rests. The city rejoices. So too, when the winds from Bruttium lash the seas, and Scylla bellows, and Charybdis hurls the sea skyward - then quiet returns. Even the Cyclops, sitting on Etna's ridge, fears his father's wrath and hides his flames. Even Laertes, watching Ithaca tremble, fears his poor kingdom might drown. But when the storm dies, the sea lies calmer than a pond. Where waves had roared, now sailboats glide. Children count fish beneath water where ships once sank.

[All lights on - stage and audience. The following is said by all people on stage as well as the Chorus through the overhead speakers]: No fate endures. Pain and joy swap places. Joy - shorter. Pain - ever waiting. One hour can overturn the world.

[Audience lights black. Stage lights on. People on stage return to movement. Nature-Sounds increase in volume.]

Chorus (Disembodied in Unison): The man who crowns your head, before whom nations kneel - he trembles too. The Medes obey him. The Indians, near Apollo's shrine, obey him. Even the Dahae and Parthian riders obey - and yet, he fears fortune's fall.

[All of the people on stage turn to the audience and say]: He sees the shifting winds, and dreads tomorrow.

[Nature-Sounds are now loud enough to force Chorus to increase volume.]

Chorus (Disembodied in Unison): You who rule life and death - lower your swollen pride. Whatever the poor man fears from you, a greater Power fears over you. Every kingdom lies under a greater one.

[All of the people on stage turn to the audience and say]: The man proud at dawn may crawl by dusk.

Chorus (Disembodied in Unison): Let no one trust too much in joy. Let no one despair of better days. Clotho, the Fate, spins all things around. She will not let Fortune stand still. She turns fate's wheel. Not even the gods grant tomorrow. All things - ours - are whirled by storm at divine speed.

[Nature-Sounds are now at a 10/10 volume - overwhelming. The stage goes black. Sound lowers to 5/10. A circular projection appears with Atreus' face.]

Atreus' Face: Who will sweep me away in whirlwind flight, wrap me in darkness, so this horror I commit cannot be seen?

[Blackout. Nature-Sounds return to a 10/10 volume. 3x Beats. Silence.]

IV. A Nightmare (627-884)

[Stage lights on. Men and Women are onstage, suspended by visible wires from the ceiling. Their bodies sway slightly, as if tugged by air or current. The Messenger enters from stage right, suspended upside-down on a wire. He spins once, his feet touch the ground, then he is lifted again - this cycle repeats throughout. As he enters, a circular projection of his face (correct orientation) appears above. The image is recognizable but blurry. When he speaks, the Messenger and his Face speak with a unified voice - one from the stage and the other from the overhead speaker.]

CHORUS: What nightmare do you bring us now?

MESSENGER (Nvntius): What place is this? Is this still Argos? Or Sparta, proud cities blessed with noble brothers? Or is it Corinth, straddling the twin seas? Or are we far away - on the banks of the savage Danube, among fleeing Alans, beneath the snow - choked sky of Hyrcania, or lost in the wilderness of the nomadic Scythians? What monstrous place is this, conscious of a deed too terrible to name?

CHORUS: Speak it. Whatever this evil is - reveal it.

[The blurry circular projection of the Messenger's Face splits onto Right and Left. On the Right - the oscillating Messenger's Face. On the Left, a new circular projection: an image this is red, blurry, shaking, and indistinct. The Messenger's Face begins to slow but then speeds up again. The Red-Projection can't be identified - it looks as though it is pulsing.]

MESSENGER: If only my mind could steady. If my body, frozen in fear, would grant release to my limbs. The image - the image of the deed is stuck in my face. Carry me far from here - beyond this maddened place - carry me like the wind carries the day when it flees this world.

CHORUS: You trap our minds in deeper fear. Tell us: What horror has you shaking? And who is the author? Not which, but which of the two? Speak - now.

[The projection of the Messenger's Face slows, but doesn't end, its oscillation. As the Messenger speaks, the people on stage are slowly lifted by the wires.]

MESSENGER: At the very peak of Pelops' palace is a southern - facing wing, its outer wall sheer as a mountain - leaning down over the city, casting shadow over the people who have long resisted their rulers. It shines - huge and gilded - its columns veined with exotic stone, bearing golden beams. That part is public. The crowd adores it. But the deeper palace, is different.

[The people on stage are visibly off the ground.]

Back behind all that splendor, the house divides, spreading into hidden wings. And buried in its lowest depth lies a sacred forbidden region - a primeval grove locked in a valley. No joyful tree grows there. No blade tends it. No fruit is found. Only yew, cypress, and black ilex float in a forest of shadows. Over it towers a single oak - ancient, proud, dominating the wood.

From this place, the House of Tantalus has always sought its signs. Here, in desperate times, they come for aid. Its roots are covered with offerings: broken trumpets, bent chariot wheels, wreckage from Myrtoan seas - spoils from every crime. Pelops' Phrygian tiara is fixed here. So is a barbarian cloak - dyed with blood - a triumph's trophy. Beneath the shadow of that oak stands a pool - still, black, as thick as Styx. It is more like the underworld than the surface of the earth. Its waters are cold, its depth unknown. They seem to bind the sky itself to sacred oaths. By night - they say the grove screams. The chains in that place rattle. The gods below moan. Spirits howl. And worse - visions. The walking dead - a whole ancient crowd - wanders out of the tombs. Wraiths mock the place with monstrous masks. Even when the sun shines, the trees burn. No flame touches them. The fires erupt from within. The forest glows red in silence. Dogs howl in threes. Apparitions seize the house. Day never ends the fear.

Night belongs to that grove. And the Religion of the Dead rules here - even at noon. This is where men go to ask the future. This is the Oracle's lair. With crashing thunder, the cave speaks. The god replies. Into that place - into that forbidden temple - Atreus dragged the sons of his brother. The altars are set. Who could describe what follows? Their noble young hands are tied behind their backs. Their heads are veiled with purple mourning bands. But still: the sacred rites are followed. The wine is poured. The salted meal is sprinkled. The blade kisses the throat. All is done in perfect ritual - so that the greatest horror might be committed rightly.

[The people on the stage are now aligned with the stage horizontally, feet going in different stage directions.]

CHORUS: Who dares to place the blade? Who is the priest of this abomination?

MESSENGER: He himself is a priest. He chants the death-curse himself, lips twisted by violence. He alone performs the rite - lays hands upon the children, positions their bodies, raises the blade. He alone observes it all. No part of the ritual is lost. The sacred grove trembles. The palace sways, the ground beneath shudders like a ship at sea, unsure where to bear its weight. A dark streak of fire tears across the sky - an omen from the left-hand air. The wine turns black, spilled upon the flames. It flows not like wine, but blood - Bacchus defiled. The royal diadem slips from his head - twice, then a third time. Even the ivory statues in the temples - they weep. The omens move all - but Atreus remains unmoved. He terrifies even the gods. Then - delay dismissed - he steps to the altar. Eyes slanted, burning - he stares. Like a tiger in the Ganges stalking two calves, uncertain which to seize - turning her jaws to this one, then that - holding back the hunger, just to taste the delay - so too does dread Atreus glare at the heads of his victims, weighing which to slaughter first. He delights in arranging the crime.

CHORUS: Which does he strike?

MESSENGER: First - (and so you do not think all pity is lost) - he offers Tantalus as the first victim.

CHORUS: And how does the boy die? What face did he wear?

MESSENGER: He stood - unafraid. He let his prayers be heard, and did not let them perish unspoken. But the beast of a man - buried the blade in his throat, pressed it in deep - his hand locked in place. Even when the sword was pulled free, the boy did not fall. He wavered, undecided - until he fell toward his uncle. Then Plisthenes - Atreus drags him to the altar, throws him beside his brother, and severs the neck. His headless body collapses forward. The severed head murmurs, a faint whimper of pain.

CHORUS: And after that? After two sons lie dead - does he spare the third? Or does he heap sin atop sin?

MESSENGER: Like a lion from Armenia, mane bristling, gorged on slaughtered cattle, resting over its kill - its mouth drenched in blood, its hunger not yet fed - so Atreus rages, his Fury still swelling. He grips the gore-soaked blade. Forgetting which son this is - he thrusts the sword one more time. Straight through - the boy receives the blade in the chest - and it bursts through his back. He falls. His blood extinguishes the altar flame. He dies from both wounds.

CHORUS: O savage crime!

MESSENGER: You shudder? If the horror ends here, Atreus is merciful.

CHORUS: Can there be more? Can nature hold a crime greater than this?

MESSENGER: You think that was the end? It was only the first step.

CHORUS: What more could he do? Throw the bodies to wild beasts? Deny them burial by flame?

MESSENGER: Would that he had let the bodies lie - unburied, unburned - left for birds and beasts to gnaw. Let them be torn, let them be foul carrion - it would have been mercy. Let the father see his children unburied.

But no. No age could believe this crime. No future will believe it.

[Projection Left shows a beating heart. On Projection Right, the Messenger's Face oscillates faster.]

He tears out the hearts still beating, veins still pulsing, the blood still warm. He handles the organs - he weighs them - he reads the veins like scrolls of fate. And once the gods are satisfied - once the omens agree - he turns with calm joy to the feast of his brother. He butchers the bodies himself. He hacks away at shoulders, arms, ribs - a butcher now. He strips them bare. He breaks the bones. Only the faces remain - and the hands once offered in trust. He spools the flesh on spits.

[Projection Left shows organs grilling.]

He sets them slowly over the coals. Juices drip from the twisted meat. The boiling cauldron roars. The fire leaps, then recoils, then leaps again, unwilling to burn this horror. The liver hisses on the spit. And I cannot say whether the flame, or the children's corpses, cried louder.

The fire turns to black smoke - and even that smoke - thick, heavy, twisted - rises not clean, but coils and clings to the very gods of the household.

[All of the people on the stage are upside down. The Projection Left is perfectly clear showing grilling organs on blood red background. Messenger's Face, Projection Right, is oscillating so fast it can't be seen. Floodlights of different colors light the stage and move across so the stage is people suspended upside down showered in multi-colors.]

MESSENGER: O Sun - if you have endurance - turn back. Drown midday in darkness. You arrived too late. A father is eating his sons. His hair is soaked with perfume. His lips stained with wine. His throat - too full for breath. He cannot swallow his joy. Only one mercy, Thyestes: you do not know. But even that mercy will soon vanish. Let Titan steer his chariot against himself. Let him smother this deed in unnatural night. Too late. All things will be revealed.

[Into the audience, Children lead Adults on leashes or bid them forwards with whips. They walk around, without noise but with threats of physical violence.]

CHORUS: Where on Earth or in Heaven has the Sun fled? Where has the light gone? Why have you turned your chariot aside? What fear drives you, Phoebus? Evening Star has not yet risen. No trumpet has yet called the third watch of night. The farmer, not yet weary, stares at this strange meal-time hour.

Why have you stopped? Has the prison of Dis burst open? Have the Giants returned to war? Has Tityos lifted his ravaged chest? Has Typhoeus rolled aside the mountain? Is the road to Phlegra being rebuilt? Are Pelion and Ossa stacked again? Have the seasons perished? Is there no more sunrise, no more sunset? Is the world broken?

Even Aurora's mother, the dew-washed goddess of first light, cannot guide the reins - nor bathe the sweaty steeds in sea. Phoebus, westward now, sees Aurora as foreign, bids the night rise - even before she is ready. But the stars refuse to light. The Moon will not manage the shadows. Oh - if only this were night! But hearts tremble. And fear rushes in. Will all fall again? Will the gods and men be crushed in another Chaos? Will sea, stars, earth - be re-swallowed by nature?

[Complete blackout. After 3x Beats, a circular projection of Men and Women wearing masks. Sound emits through overhead speaker.]

No more the guiding Sun - no more the seasons. No more Sol to mark summer from winter. No more Moon to conquer her brother's light. The gods collapse. The zodiac falls. The Ram leaps into the sea. The Bull and Twins are dragged down. The Lion - burning - crashes to Earth. The Virgin, abandoned, follows. Libra, with its justice, and the deadly Scorpion - all fall. Sagittarius loses his bow. The Goat shatters his jar. Pisces are the last to go - and the Bears, who never touched the sea, are drowned. The Snake, divider of the Bears, slithers down. The cold northern pole cracks. Arctophylax - the guardian - falls from his post.

[Blackout. 3x Beats. Stage lights on. Full of people. They all speak in unison.]

Chorus (Embodied Collective: And what of us? Why have we been chosen to survive the collapse? Why are we the last age? We who have lost the Sun - or driven him out? Let no one lament. Let no one fear. Who clings to life when the world itself is dying?

[Blackout.]

V. And What of Us? (885-1031)

[Stage lights rise slowly. On the backstage wall, a projection of the sun rising in the west and sets in the east — completing a full cycle every 30 seconds. Center-stage is a circular revolve, spinning counter-clockwise. Front-stage, on a low bench, sits Thyestes, back facing the audience. He eats at a simple table with visible delight. Back-stage, Atreus stands elevated on a darkened platform, watching. Two Circular Face projections hover above: Thyestes' Face to stage left; Atreus' Face to stage right. When either speaks, their voice is emitted through overhead speakers.]

[As the lights settle, Thyestes eats and his projected Face is full of shining color and contentment. Eating Sounds - chewing, sipping, and quiet sighs of delight - coming from the stage are amplified through side speakers. Atreus, on his platform above Thyestes, can't contain his happiness. He is jumping up and down. Punching the sky. Turning around. Dancing. Atreus' Face is awash in golden color and is spinning in circles with a look of contented post-coital ecstasy.]

Atreus: I rise - equal to the stars.

[Atreus falls to his knees and weeps.]

Above all men, I stride with a head that touches heaven. Now I hold the royal glory. Now I sit on my father's throne.

[He rises and makes a gesture which causes servants to appear and bring Thyestes new dishes to try. As the servants enter the stage with new dishes, Men and Women enter the audience grilling different meats and offering them.]

The gods may go. I have surpassed every prayer. It is enough - more than enough. Even I am full.

[Atreus stands over Thyestes' with unconstrained glee. Atreus' Face becomes normal and begins speaking. On stage, Atreus is pantomiming plotting.]

Atreus' Face: But why stop here? I shall go further. My brother's children are dead. Let shame no longer hold me back. The day has fled - now, act while the sky is empty.

[On stage, Atreus is continuing to plot with unconstrained happiness. At the same time, the projection of Atreus' Face and the sounds emitting from overhead speakers becomes unconstrained with rage.]

If only I could trap the fleeing gods - drag them back, make them witness this avenging feast. Let all see it. But if not all, then at least our father - let Tantalus behold. Even if Day itself resists, I will tear through the dark and show you, Thyestes, the shadows that hide your ruin.

[Atreus' Face calms and speaks angrily but with precision.]

You've dined too long in peace. Too long with a happy face. Enough wine. Enough meat. Now, sobriety is required.

[Atreus straightens and makes a gesture. A servant appears. Atreus' Face looks on in anticipation, wondering what will happen.]

Atreus: Servants! Open the temple doors. Let the Festal House be revealed. Let me see him - his face as he looks upon the heads of his children. What colors will flood it? What words will grief force from him? Will he fall stiff - silent - as the soul flies from him? This is my harvest. Not to see him weep - but to watch as he

becomes a man worthy of weeping. Open the chambers -
bright with torchlight.

*[The stage darkens and spotlights appear on Atreus
and Thyestes.]*

He reclines, still drenched in gold and purple. His
wine-heavy head rests against his arm.

He belches.

*[The circular projection of Ateus' Face disappears
and the word "Vincō!" appears and confetti falls from the
ceiling as the audience hears Atreus' voice from the
overhead speaker scream the words "I win." Atreus' Face
reappears awash in golden color, spinning in circles, with
a look of contented post-coital ecstasy.]*

O gods above! I am greater than you.

A king above kings.

My prayers have been outdone.

*[Atreus falls and weeps in uncontrollable joy. Atreus'
Face becomes steady and is hard and angry.]*

He drains the wine - the wine flows red in silver
bowls capacious as basins - but drink! Drink more!
There's still blood to hide. Let old wine cover it. Let the
final cup be raised. Let the father drink the blood of his
sons - as he would have drunk mine. Listen - he sings! He
toasts! He's lost control.

*[Blackout - except for Atreus' and Thyestes' Face
projections. Spotlight on Thyestes. The revolve has
stopped spinning and is situated so that Thyestes faces the*

audience. The Eating Sounds emitting from side speakers increases in volume so it is background to the voice emitting from the overhead speakers. Thyestes' Face is pure contented trust, faith, and enjoyment.]

Thyestes' Face: O heart, dulled by long griefs - set aside your burdens. Let sorrow go. Let fear go. Let exile's gray companion, poverty and shame, fall away. It matters not from where you fell - only where you stand now.

[Thyestes calls a servant for more food and wine. When the servant fills his plate and cup, he speaks.]

Thyestes: Great it is - from so high a ruin - to plant your steps again on solid ground. Great it is - beneath a broken crown - to hold your neck upright, to carry ruin like a noble, ruined king.

[The servant has taken away dishes and cups. Thyestes returns to eating and drinking.]

Thyestes' Face: But now, away with clouds of fate! Let memory vanish. Let smiles return. Forget Thyestes. It is the curse of the miserable never to believe in joy. Even if Fortune smiles - they are too wounded to smile back.

[Thyestes jerks and looks around as if hearing something. He drinks a large gulp of wine. He shrugs and returns to eating.]

Thyestes' Face: Why do you summon me back? Why do you forbid me from celebrating this day? Why do you demand tears? There is no cause! Why stop me from wreathing my hair in flowers?

[Thyestes again jerks, looks around, and drinks more wine.]

But - stop! Stop! My brow - just crowned with roses - now shivers. My hair - heavy with perfume - stands on end. A sob breaks mid-song. Rain falls from unwilling eyes. Grief is a habit for the wretched. Tears are beloved to those who have wept too long. Yes - I long to cry. To send forth curses. To rip my robe, to wail like a beast.

[Thyestes again jerks, looks around, and drinks more wine.]

Something stirs - a foretaste of future grief. My mind shudders. A storm brews before the wind. What griefs do I imagine? What chaos do I fear? Madness! - No.

[Thyestes suddenly stands with a full cup of wine and shouts drunkenly]

Thyestes: Trust your brother. Whatever it is, it's nothing - or too late to dread.

[Draining the cup, he sits and returns to eating.]

Thyestes' Face: But I - I do not want misfortune. And yet - some fear roams my chest. Tears fall - without cause. Is it pain? Or fear? Or does great joy also have tears?

[Blackout.]

[Stage lights on. A large comfort room full of cushions and servants waving fans. The two circular Face projections - Thyestes' Face is content on a background of light blue and Atreus' Face with contained glee on gold -

are on the backstage wall. Thyestes lies on large cushions, and is fanned by servants. Atreus, with wires attached, enters stage-right. As he does, children enter the audience and serve wine.]

Atreus: Come, brother - let us celebrate this day together as one. This is the day that seals my rule, the day that binds the scepter firm, the day that locks in peace - forever.

Thyestes: I'm full from the feast - and from Bacchus no less. But one joy could crown it all: to share this happiness with my sons.

[Atreus lifts from the ground and Atreus' Face glows.]

Atreus: Believe this, then - your sons are here, in their father's arms.

[At this point, while Thyestes engages Atreus, the color around Thyestes' Face shifts and becomes darker and the facial expression becomes more concerned.]

Here now. Here always. No part of them will be taken from you. I will give you the faces you long for. Your house will be filled with children. You'll have your fill. Fear not. Now, mixed among mine, they grace the feast with youthful charm. But they shall be summoned. Take the cup - filled with ancestral wine.

[Atreus is literally flying around the stage.]

Thyestes: I take it - a gift from my brother's table. May this wine be poured to our father's gods. Now let it be drunk.

[The color around Thyestes' Face has become black and the facial expression bewildered. Thyestes is unable to lift his cup.]

Thyestes' Face: But - what? My hands refuse. The weight grows heavy. It drags down my arm. The wine - it leaps back from my lips. It flees my mouth, runs cold across my face. Even the table shudders beneath me. The light dims - the very air, caught between day and night, hangs stunned. What is this? The heavens falter, shaken. The sky buckles. Thick darkness presses in, night hiding inside night. Every star has fled.

[Thyestes turns toward Atreus. His voice pleads.]

Thyestes: Whatever this is - I pray my brother and my sons be spared. Let every storm strike this worthless head. Just - give me back my sons!

Atreus: You shall have them. No day shall ever take them from you again.

[Thyestes' Face begins to weep.]

Thyestes: What madness stirs within me? What trembles through my chest? This weight is not mine. My body groans - but not in my voice. Come, sons - come close. Your father calls. Come now - seeing you will cure this pain. But - what voices answer?

Atreus: Open your arms, father. They have come. Do you recognize your sons?

Thyestes: I see - my brother.

[Thyestes collapses into himself on a cushion. Thyestes' Face gains control.]

Thyestes' Face: Earth - can you endure this crime? Why do you not split open, swallow him whole - tear down your roof and hurl all Mycenae into the abyss? We should be standing before Tantalus now. Let the hinges of hell be ripped apart. Let a valley deeper than Tartarus open. Let birds gnaw his entrails - and mine. Bury us in Acheron. Above us, let guilty souls float, disembodied heads drift, and let Phlegethon scorch the sand with fire as it floods even our exile. And yet - you remain still, Earth. Weightless. Worthless.

[Thyestes regains his composure. He stares at Atreus.]

Thyestes: The gods have fled.

Atreus: But no - take them now. You've waited so long. There's no delay, not even from your brother. Enjoy them. Kiss them. Divide their embraces among the three.

[Thyestes stands and faces Atreus. Thyestes' Face is full of wrath.]

Thyestes: This is peace? This is grace? This is a brother's faith? You call this forgiveness?

[Thyestes' Face becomes pleading.]

I ask nothing, not even to have my sons alive. Just - let me bury them. Give me what remains - I'll burn it. I do not ask as a father who will keep them. Only one who must lose them.

[The glow around Atreus' Face intensifies and it takes on a look of ecstasy.]

Atreus: Whatever of your sons still exists - you have it. Whatever does not - you have it still.

[Thyestes stills. Thyestes' Face weeps.]

Thyestes: Are they cast to wild birds, torn by beaks? Or saved for beasts? Or fed to savage jaws?

[Atreus calls in servants. They bring in empty plates and cookware.]

Atreus: You yourself have feasted - on your children's unholy flesh.

[Thyestes looks at the dishes he used and pots he was served. The color around Thyestes' Face becomes blood red and the facial expression becomes Knowing.]

Thyestes: This is the deed that made the sun retreat - this is what shamed the gods and drove the day back to its birth.

[Thyestes collapses onto the stage.]

Thyestes' Face: What cries can I utter? What laments are equal? What words - what words - can contain such horror?

I see the severed heads, *[three severed head fall from wires]*

the torn-off hands, *[three sets of torn-off hands fall from wires]*

the broken stumps where legs once stood *[three sets of legs]*

- this is what the father's hunger could not hold.

[*Thyestes' Face oscillates until the circular projection is a pure blood red blur. Thyestes stands.*]

Thyestes: Inside me, my guts heave. The crime writhes, sealed inside. It has no exit. [*He speaks to a servant.*] Give me a sword - (though it already drinks my blood) - let there be a way for my children to pass through me.

[*The servant looks at Thyestes, looks at Atreus, and runs away.*]

Thyestes: No sword? Then let my chest echo with the bruising of my fists.

[*Thyestes punches the air and breaks down crying.*]

Thyestes Face: Hold your hand, poor wretch. Let us honor the dead. Who has ever seen such a crime? Who among the Heniochi on the harsh cliffs of inhospitable Caucasus? Who, even Procrustes in Cecropian lands? A father... pressing down his children - and by them, pressed.

[*Thyestes rises and faces Atreus.*]

Thyestes: Is there no limit to crime?

Atreus: There's a limit to doing crime - not to avenging it.

[*Stage darkens except for Atreus' Face which is surrounded by blood red.*]

Atreus' Face: Even this is too little for me. I should have poured their hot blood straight from their wounds into your open mouth, so you would drink not just their flesh, but the life still pulsing.

[Full stage lights come on and audience lights flash on. Stage darkens except for Atreus' Face.]

Atreus' Face: Those were words spoken in haste, in anger.

[Shaking himself, Atreus is on a platform above Thyestes. The platform is surrounded by servants. While the following is spoken, Thyestes' Face oscillates into pure blur.]

Atreus: Instead, I struck them myself, slaughtered them on sacred altars, appeased the hearth with votive blood, hacked their bodies, sliced their limbs into parts - boiled some in bubbling bronze, roasted others on slow flames. I cut them while they still breathed, watched their guts groan as I skewered them alive, carried flame in my own hands. Ah - their father could have done it better.

Atreus' Face: My rage was wasted: he chewed their flesh with impious mouth - but unknowing. And they died - unknowing.

[Thyestes has fallen on the stage sobbing.]

Thyestes: O wandering seas shut in by shores - hear this crime. You too, gods - wherever you have fled - and gods below, hear this. Earth, hear this. Heavy Night, hear this. You, with your black cloud, you alone remain. Only you see me, only you pity me. (And you - without stars.) I will not pray for myself. There's nothing left to ask. But let my prayers serve others.

[As Thyestes rises the stage darkens. He speaks facing the audience in a spotlight.]

Thyestes: You - lord of heaven, ruler of the vaulted sky - wrap the world in stormclouds, let the winds clash in war, let your thunder crack from every side! But not with your lesser hand, the one you use to strike homes and roofbeams. No - use the hand that shattered triple-peaked mountains, the hand that felled the giants who stood beside mountains - use that arm. Hurl fire. Avenge the vanished sun. Fill the stolen daylight with thunderbolts.

[He pauses in a pose pleading with the gods.]

Thyestes' Face: Don't hesitate - if justice is to fall on one, let it fall on both. If not both - then let it fall on me. Strike me down. Through this heart, drive your triple-tongued flame. If I would give my children to fire - let me burn too. If no god moves, if no divine hand reaches for its spear, then let night remain forever. Let darkness cover this endless crime. I make no complaint, Titan, if you never rise again.

[Atreus is flying around the stage.]

Atreus: Now I praise my hands. Now I hold my true victory. My crime would have been lost if you had not suffered so. Now - I believe I have children. Now - I believe my marriage bed was faithful.

Thyestes: What did the children do to deserve this?

Atreus: They were yours.

Thyestes: To give a father his children -

Atreus: Yes - and I rejoice that they were certainly yours.

Thyestes: Gods who protect the just - I call you as witnesses!

Atreus: Why not call on your wife?

Thyestes: Can crime undo crime?

Atreus: I know what pains you: not the evil meal you ate, but that you didn't plan it. You're not horrified at the feast - you're angry it wasn't yours. You meant to prepare a banquet just like this - serve it to your brother, with your wife's help, your children's death on the menu. Only one thing stopped you: you thought they were yours.

[Atreus calls for a servant who brings him a sword with a giant circle hilt.]

Thyestes: The gods will come. They will avenge. My prayers deliver you to their justice.

Atreus: And I deliver you - to your sons for punishment.

[Atreus plunges the sword into Thyestes chest up to the circle hilt.]

CURTAIN